YOU KNOW YOU'RE A
DOG LOVER
WHEN...

BEN FRASER

summersdale

YOU KNOW YOU'RE A DOG LOVER WHEN…

First published in 2010
This edition copyright © Summersdale Publishers Ltd, 2017

Illustrations by Roger Penwill

An Hachette UK Company
www.hachette.co.uk

Summersdale Publishers Ltd
Part of Octopus Publishing Group Limited
Carmelite House
50 Victoria Embankment
LONDON
EC4Y 0DZ
UK

www.summersdale.com

Printed and bound in China

ISBN: 978-1-84953-982-1

Substantial discounts on bulk quantities of Summersdale books are available to corporations, professional associations and other organisations. For details contact general enquiries: telephone: +44 (0) 1243 771107 or email: enquiries@summersdale.com.

TO.................................

FROM............................

The dog has his OWN PLACE at the dining table so he can eat with the family.

Your mobile ringtone is
'Who Let the Dogs Out?'

You always
CO-ORDINATE YOUR OUTFIT
to match your mutt's – who
said dog collars aren't in?

You've been on so many
LONG-DISTANCE WALKIES
that your dog rivals Bear
Grylls in tackling extreme
outdoor conditions.

You don't mind that your
dog has more friends
than you on Facebook.

Your prized
possession is your
NOVELTY TELEPHONE:
a dog and bone, of course!

You spend hours
searching the website
Muttmatcher.com
to locate your
PERFECT CANINE COMPANION.

You bribe the judges at Crufts so you can take their front-row seats and be closest to the action.

You count
BOUNCING PUPPIES
instead of sheep to
fall asleep at night.

You spend hours training for DOG AGILITY COMPETITIONS – even on your pooch's day off.

You believe that fine art has its place, but insist that there's nothing finer than a picture of a bulldog and his pals playing pool.

The most expensive
things in your house are
the 2,000-count EGYPTIAN
COTTON SHEETS on
which your dog sleeps.

You save all of your dog's fur – to knit into a STYLISH JUMPER.

You spend hours grooming
– you occasionally run a comb
through your own hair,
but you and your dog both
know who the looker is.

You refuse to wear
patterned clothes unless
they are houndstooth – well,
except for your pyjamas
with cute little bones on.

You do your bit for canine–
human equality by holding a
CHARITY DOGSLED RACE,
where the owners pull huskies
on sleds through the snow.

You have the Kennel
Club down as your
EMERGENCY CONTACT
NUMBER.

You have taken on enough rescue dogs to become a serious rival to Battersea Dogs & Cats Home.

You own more
TENNIS BALLS
than Andy Murray.

You write to the council demanding that they install a dog loo with separate cubicles in your local park – after all, a dog has its dignity to consider.

You start a CANINE-THEMED
CD COLLECTION for your
dog, which includes
David Bowie's *Diamond
Dogs*, Ozzy Osbourne's
Bark at the Moon and
everything by Wolfmother.

You can trace your
DOG'S FAMILY TREE
further back than your own.

You realise you are not so much the dog whisperer as the dog yodeller, after your prized Alsatian runs amok in the park.

You have

PREMIUM PET INSURANCE

which covers your dog
for the emotional strain
of excessive moulting.

Your neighbours
are alarmed at the
AMOUNT OF BONES
in your back garden
and alert the police.

You arrive on holiday and immediately call your dogsitter and have them put Fido on the phone so you can tell him just how much 'Mummy' and 'Daddy' are missing him.

You have subscriptions to all the MUST-HAVE MONTHLIES – *Dog World*, *Puppy Dog Tales* and, of course, *Chihuahua Connection* magazine.

You have over two decades' worth of 'autographs' from the *BLUE PETER* DOGS.

Your DVD collection consists exclusively of movies in which dogs share star billing – Tom Hanks and a slobbering French Mastiff, what's not to like?!

You perch on the
arm of your sofa instead
of getting your dog to
move... they just look too
CUTE AND COMFORTABLE.

You watched so much *Lassie* growing up that if you hear a Collie barking you immediately run to the local police station to report a suspected 'BOY-DOWN-A-WELL' SCENARIO.

You have an obedience ring – and make family members sit in it.

Your dog has their own travel arrangements in first class, as well as their own PLATINUM FREQUENT FLYER CLUB CARD.

Family Christmas cards
feature only the four-legged
family members wearing
SANTA HATS AND LITTLE
BLACK BOOTIES.

You always request 'Roll Over, Beethoven' by Chuck Berry at discos, and proceed to imitate a St Bernard doing just that in the middle of the dance floor.

Over half your garden
is taken up by the
LUXURY KENNEL you
built for your star canine
– complete with bone-
shaped paddling pool.

You spend so much money
on ORGANIC DOG FOOD
the company makes you
its chief shareholder.

Your friends think you've turned into a West Coast gangster since you've started using the phrase ''Sup, dawg?' on a regular basis.

You SERENADE YOUR DOG
at dinner time every night,
à la *Lady and the Tramp*.

Your partner buys you
PERSONALISED DOG TAGS
for Valentine's Day.

You're so handy with your pooper scooper that you've earned the nickname 'The Va-poo-riser'.

You firmly believe
that cats are actually a
LESSER FORM OF CANINE
which, thanks to their
haughty nature, failed
to evolve any further.

You know the name of
every dog you pass on
the canal during walkies,
but fail to recognise
any of their owners.

Your friends refuse
to get in your car as they
know they will come out
LOOKING LIKE A YETI
from the build-up of
Rex's hair in the back.

You love long walks by the beach and sharing an ice cream while watching the sun go down – with your perfect pooch, obviously.

You refer to your closest
friends as 'YOUR PACK'.

You go shopping for
a SPECIAL BIRTHDAY
OUTFIT... for your dog.

Your colleagues ask about your nearest and dearest and you immediately show them the framed photos of SIR FLUFFY BARKINGTON III featured in pride of place on your desk.

You become fascinated
with astronomy after you
discover the Dog Star.

You splash out on a PAMPERED PAWS SPA DAY for your pooch's birthday.

You always cause trouble,
because you just can't
let sleeping dogs lie.

Your neighbours
refuse to speak to you
after seeing the way you
`MARKED YOUR TERRITORY`
on either side of your garden.

You spend the whole day
CUDDLING THE DOG
whenever you are hungover,
but feel the 'hair of the dog'
is not quite as effective
as people make out.

You devote your free time
to finding more interesting
ways to present your
dog's dinner, although
kibble en croûte didn't go
down too well last time.

One of your favourite
pastimes is recreating
FAMOUS FILM SCENES
with your canine co-star.

You use your Nicky Clarke style album to create fabulous new looks for your pooch.

You have a habit of
ABSENTLY PATTING YOUR
CHILDREN on the head.

Canine yoga is your
NEW FAVOURITE
HOBBY, which includes
such positions as 'The Ear
Scratch' and 'Watering
the Lamp post'.

You haven't read a letter or newspaper in the past decade which hasn't been well-ventilated with teeth marks.

You are frequently
seen carrying your
PRECIOUS PUP around in
a baby sling, making
comments like 'Who's
Mummy's little precious?'
in a mushy voice.

You own every SPANIEL-THEMED ceramic plate known to man, along with Spaniel-themed cushion covers, mugs, key rings and a personalised 'I Love Spaniels' T-shirt.

You start telling people
that your bark is worse
than your bite.

Someone says they
think you look fetching
and you immediately
go and RETRIEVE THE
NEAREST STICK.

You are disappointed to discover that, aside from the star's shaggy haircut, *Dog the Bounty Hunter* has very little to do with canines or their owners.

After staring into
your dog's eyes for hours
on end you are beginning
to believe you have a
TELEPATHIC LINK
with your pooch.

You've been banned from
group sports because you
like to PLAY 'RUFF'.

You take your pooch to the park so often you know exactly what it is to be 'dog tired'.

You refer to those extra
few pounds you've been
carrying for years as
'PUPPY FAT' – you must
give up those doggy treats!

Your favourite pub is
the DOG AND DUCK.

You hold classes for water-shy canines: 'The Art of Doggy-paddling.'

You have an inexplicable dislike for the postman and CAN'T RESIST GROWLING if you see him pass by.

If you're interested in finding
out more about our books,
find us on Facebook at
SUMMERSDALE PUBLISHERS
and follow us on Twitter at
@SUMMERSDALE.

WWW.SUMMERSDALE.COM